How to become
D0505363

FUEL[RCA]

Royal College of Art
3 8021 00860596 8

Other titles from
Centre for Strategy and Communication

Taking and writing minutes
Jan Burnell

Moving into management
Julia Braggins

How to become a brilliant presenter

Tess Woodcraft

Centre for Strategy and Communication

Centre for Strategy and Communication
Centre for Strategy and Communication is a centre for reflection and change.

We help individuals and organisations in the public and non profit sectors transform the way they communicate. We work with individuals to find their best personal presentation style, and with organisations to find the unique voice that reflects their values and builds their reputation.

If you would like more information about the Centre's consultancy and training you can find our website on www.the-centre.co.uk
Or contact us on 020 7490 3030

First published 2004 by
Centre for Strategy and Communication
140 Old Street, London EC1V 9BW

ISBN 0–9546315–1–X

Cartoons: Mike Turner

Produced for the Centre for Strategy and Communication by
Chase Publishing Services, Fortescue, Sidmouth, EX10 9QG
Printed in the European Union

Contents

Acknowledgements

This book is a compilation of the wisdom, advice and experience of all the presentation skills trainers at the Centre for Strategy and Communication. Although my name is on the cover, I have been lucky to work with such a talented team and I owe them a big debt.

The book also brings together tips and advice that trainees themselves have brought to presentation skills training. One of the great things about presentation skills training is that as a trainer, you always learn new things at every session! Again, many, many thanks.

Tess Woodcraft

Introduction

Most of us have attended a conference and been impressed by a speaker who held the audience's attention, was clear, warm and inspiring. A memorable presenter. One who stood out from the crowd and brought the subject matter to life.

You can be that presenter.

These days almost everyone needs to be able to give a good presentation. Whether you are representing your organisation at a meeting or a pitch, or whether you are applying for a new job – you want to feel confident that you can persuade and energise your audience.

This book will help you think through how to prepare, how to assemble and structure your content and, perhaps most important of all, how to overcome your nerves and give a confident, professional and high impact presentation. It will help you enjoy giving presentations.

1 What you need to know before you start to develop your presentation

Preparation is at the heart of an effective presentation.

Before you even begin to develop your presentation, you will need to find out who the audience is and what is expected of you.

Basic details (who, what, why, where, when?)

When you are asked to give a presentation make sure you know:

Who? Who is going to be there, how big the audience is likely to be, what they expect? (see more on audience below)

What? What is the event? What is your brief? What is the title of your presentation? What will you be expected to cover? Who else is speaking – where do you fit in? If there are other speakers, is it a debate, are all speakers exploring different aspects of the same theme? What type of presentation is expected (keynote, workshop, lecture etc.). Will they need a copy of your presentation (by what date?)?

Why? Why have they asked you to speak (rather than someone else)? What is the purpose of the event, why is it being held?

Where? Where is it being held? The address (and do you need a map, travelling instructions to get there?). What is the layout of the room, will you be able to change it? Tell the organisers if you need any special facilities.

When? When is the date and time of the presentation? Will there be other presentations, earlier in the event, that you should have heard before giving your presentation? How long are you expected to speak for? Will there be questions?

Your audience

Find out as much as you can about your audience, for example:

- Men/women
- Cultural issues/language
- Age
- Socio-economic group(s)
- Why are they going to be attending? What do they expect? What do they need from you?
- Experience of the issues
- Preconceived ideas about the issues
- Did they specifically ask for you to be a speaker? If so, why?
- Are there any particular people in the audience you should know about?
- Dress code?

Remember the pecking order – the audience is more important than you. They can choose to accept or reject what you say, and you want them to accept!

The aims of the event

Find out as much as you can about the event itself.

- What is this event/meeting/conference for?
- What should it achieve?
- Will everyone attending have the same 'agenda'?
- Is it part of a regular cycle of events or is it a one-off?

2
Content

What is your aim?

You will need to decide what you want to achieve with your presentation.

For example:

- Do you want to get the audience to take action?
- Do you want them to think differently about an important issue?
- Do you want to encourage or enthuse?
- Do you want to position your organisation as the leading body in its field?

Be clear about your aim before you start marshalling your arguments and putting together your supporting evidence.

Then ask yourself – how can I achieve this aim? What do I need to do, and what do I need to say to achieve this aim?

In achieving your aims you will need to bear in mind:

- The aims/needs of your audience
- The limitations of time and understanding of your audience (how realistic is your aim?)

If you are clear about your aim, you should find it relatively easy to identify your messages – what does the audience need to hear, what do they need to take on board?

Messages

If you are not clear about your messages, then your audience can't be expected to work them out.

Clear messages will help your audience follow your presentation, and grasp what you want to get across to them. Messages help your audience *understand*. If you simply give your audience lots of information, they will get lost in the detail – your messages help them to process the information.

Your messages are at the heart of what you want to convey. Ask yourself:

- What is my big idea?
- What are the key points I want to get across?
- What do I want my audience to remember in six months' time?
- What do I want my audience to do?

A message is usually a position, an argument, an idea, a point of view. Very occasionally it is a big fact that is capable of changing people's perception of a problem.

There are two ranks of messages – overarching messages, and key messages.

Overarching messages

An overarching message is the very big idea that underpins everything you and your organisation say. It provides a context. It helps your audience understand where you are coming from. It is likely that your overarching message will be the same for a wide range of presentations.

Example
A health minister might decide that his/her overarching message is that the health service must modernise – the British people need a twenty-first century health service.

This would be an important underpinning idea whether today's speech is about waiting lists, expensive drugs, nurse shortages or hospital cleaning.

Key messages

Key messages are the main arguments you are bringing forward on the particular subject you are talking about today. Confine yourself to just two or three key messages.

Our health minister, talking about waiting lists, might have three key messages:

We need to:

- Modernise the systems
- Modernise the culture
- Modernise the training of our people

Or on expensive drugs he/she might have the following key messages:

We've got to understand:

- What people need – people's aspirations are rising, can we keep pace?
- What works – NICE is an effective body evaluating the claims for drugs
- What we can afford – the NHS is not a bottomless pit

Having determined your key messages, you need to back them up. You cannot make unsubstantiated assertions. The audience needs you to provide evidence for your views.

Back up your messages with:

- Facts. Be very selective, an important part of preparation is deciding what to leave out. The audience are not going to have to sit an exam afterwards – they don't need to be swamped with detail!
- Examples – stories, anecdotes, illustrations (we remember more of what we see than of what we hear, so paint a picture – get us to SEE what you are talking about)
- History/context – you may need to give us some background to the current situation (but don't get bogged down in it)
- Third party endorsement – if Nelson Mandela or a team of scientists from Cambridge University back up what you say, then tell us!

Example

Key message: we need tougher laws if we are to eliminate the pay gap between men and women.

Facts: Women earn 80% of men's earnings. Over her lifetime, this will cost the average woman half a million pounds.

History: The Equal Pay Act is now over 30 years old. In that 30 years we have seen women's pay go up (in 1971 women earned 60% of men's wages). But over the past ten years we have seen no significant shift – it has been stuck at 80% for ten years.

Example: Let's look at supermarket cashiers. Think of the last time you were in your local supermarket. Their pay is amongst the lowest in the country and yet they have enormous boredom stress, responsibility for customer care, and danger because they handle money. 90% of cashiers are women.

Third party endorsement: The Equal Opportunities Commission has said that the pay gap is their top priority – without equal pay women can never hope to fulfil their potential.

Language

- Simple – not simplistic
- Adding oomph to your language
- Warm words
- Avoiding jargon

Simple – not simplistic

Try to make your language clear and simple. Presenting is *verbal* communication so the audience has to be able to absorb information fast. They can't go back over your text to puzzle out the meaning of a sentence or phrase. It has to mean something as soon as they hear it.

Don't use long, convoluted words in an effort to impress your audience. Try to avoid passive verbs – be active. Be confident. Simplicity and immediacy have impact.

Don't say:

'Celebrations and felicitations are due to our estimable organisation on this day, the first of July.'

Do say:

'Today is a big day for our organisation.'

The simpler the language, the more quickly we can grasp the meaning. Using simple language is not the same as being simplistic. Don't patronise your audience. Don't talk down.

Adding oomph to your language

A few dramatic adjectives will add a touch of excitement and emphasis to your presentation.

Don't say:
'Tired'

Do say:
'Shattered'

But be careful, you don't want to be accused of overstating your case, or using unnecessarily flowery language. Some of your audience will want you to be a bit dramatic, others will want a more measured, down to earth approach. So ring the changes.

Warm words

Warm words are words that attract us, that warm us. By using 'warm words' you can get your audience feeling good about you and what you are saying (see Chapter 8).

Jargon

Avoid jargon at all costs. It baffles and alienates your audience. And it is much more prevalent in all our conversations than we usually realise.

- Acronyms and abbreviations – watch out for TWPs and FWPs! (Three Word Phrases, Four Word Phrases etc.). Even abbreviations that are widely used in your world will be puzzling to others, e.g. HA can be Health Authority or Housing Association
- Shortenings – e.g. 'vol orgs' (most people don't know what voluntary organisations are, let alone 'vol orgs')
- Technical terms – you might assume that 'everybody knows' what technical terms or phrases used in your world

mean, but everybody doesn't know. Some examples of technical terms are:

  - 'Voids' – a housing professionals' term for empty properties
  - The voluntary sector/voluntary organisations also known as NGOs, non-profits, charities
  - Evidence based

- In-jokes – a presentation should be inclusive, not excluding. Be very wary of in-jokes (even if you think everyone in the room is in on the joke)
- Job titles – if you are going to use job titles in your talk, make sure you explain the purpose and, where necessary, the seniority of the role. Lots of people don't know the difference in rank between an Army Major and a Commander; or don't know whether a Civil Service Grade 3 is higher or lower than a Grade 5. One organisation's project manager is another organisation's account director
- Phrases that put you in a box – there are lots of phrases that 'fix' you in the audience's mind as different from them
  - 'New Labour' phrases, e.g. 'scoping', 'a raft of measures', 'rolling out' – these words and phrases are rarely used in more traditional organisations (beware,

there are lots of words like this associated with the government's newer initiatives)

- Class-related words and phrases, e.g. 'rugger' rather than 'rugby'
- Management-speak, e.g. 'downsizing', 'performance indicators'

Tip for simpler language

Think about the way you would present to a friend or relative. Someone you respect, but someone who is no expert on your subject. You certainly would not want to patronise them, but you'd need to talk in clear, jargon free, conversational language.

Soundbites

'Soundbites' make your ideas memorable.

A soundbite is a fairly short (15–30 second) phrase which sums up your message in a memorable way. Soundbites can be used to good effect in the body of the presentation or as a strong closing, especially if you are going to press release the speech.

Your preparation time should include thinking up some effective soundbites. But don't overdo soundbites. Too many and you sound very clichéd.

Some soundbites rely on 'big words', some on rhetoric and repetition, others rely on audience identification, others are arresting puns.

'Big words'

Using larger than life, conversational words can have a big impact. For example:

- 'huge' or 'massive' rather than 'large'
- 'impact' rather than 'effect'
- 'drenched' rather than 'wet'

Rhetoric and repetition

Trebles – repeating the same word three times:

- 'Oversexed. Overpaid. Over here.'
- 'Education, education, education.'
- 'Bonded labour robs children of their education, it robs them of their childhood and it robs them of their future.'

Emphasising the repeated word is essential to make a success of using trebles.

Doubles work in the same way ('Tough on crime, tough on the causes of crime'), but they are more difficult to deliver.

Audience identification

Using references or phrases that the audience will recognise and relate to:

- 'William Hague, you are the weakest link, goodbye.' (Tony Blair, 2001)
- 'Watch my lips, no new taxes.'
- 'As my 13-year-old daughter might say, that's a wicked idea!'
- 'All I can say to that is, Elvis is alive and well and sunning himself by a pool in Argentina!'

Plays on words

Metaphors, similes, puns and chiasmus can all form the basis of effective soundbites – but make sure you can deliver them effectively, with confidence.

Metaphors:

- 'The government is asking us to jump onto broken glass in our bare feet.'
- 'Transport chiefs are developing the new road policy from behind the windscreen of a car.'

Similes:

- 'He had a smile like a Cheshire cat.'

Puns:

- 'He's been sitting on the fence for so long, he has splinters in his backside.'

Chiasmus:

- 'It's not the men in my life, but the life in my men.' (Mae West)
- 'You can take the girl out of the city, but you can't take the city out of the girl.'

3
Structure

The most robust structure for a presentation looks like this:

Attention grabber

↓

The Three Tell-ums

↓

Strong close

Grabbing attention

The first three minutes of your presentation are the key to success. In your preparation, spend some time thinking about an attention grabbing opener. This opening should set the scene and embody your main message. It should be lively, dramatic and memorable.

Deliver your opener with confidence. A strong opening delivered with confidence sends lots of positive subliminal messages (e.g. you are someone who has made a real effort so your audience feel valued; you have flair; you are a lateral thinker).

Here are some possibilities:

- Quote
- Joke
- Props 1 – real props
- Props 2 – symbolic/metaphor props
- Picture/video/sound tape
- Party, party
- Visualisation

- Question
- Statistic

(See Chapter 4 – Attention Grabbing Openings.)

The Three Tell-ums

The 'Three Tell-ums' provide the basic backbone structure for your talk.

First Tell-um – Tell them what you are going to tell them

Second Tell-um – Tell them

Third Tell-um – Tell them what you have just told them

First Tell-um – Tell them what you are going to tell them

You tell the audience, briefly, what your presentation will cover.

The First Tell-um provides a framework for your talk. It is like giving your audience a map, and saying, 'This is where we are going today.' A clear First Tell-um helps them to follow the logic of your argument, to see where you are going and feel secure.

The First Tell-um will include:

- Your overarching message (which provides the context and aids understanding)
- Your two, three or four key messages

Each of your key messages should be backed up with a couple of amplifying sentences. Don't just list your key messages. This would be too condensed for your audience to take in. On the other hand, don't go on and on giving additional information about your key messages at this stage (because then there would be no distinction between your First and Second Tell-um, and that would be very confusing).

Example of First Tell-um
'Global warming is probably the single most important problem facing mankind [overarching message] + Rivers and seas will rise,

weather patterns will change and droughts and floods will ravage the planet [brief amplification].'

'Tonight I want to talk to you about the Kyoto Accord and why it is an important blueprint for change at a macro level [key message 1] – many countries signed the Accord in 2000, negotiations were hard, it is not perfect, but it is our only hope of change [brief amplification].'

'Then I want to go on to look at the micro level – what all of us here in this room can do [key message 2]. In particular I want to look at exciting new developments in waste management in a handful of local authority areas which demonstrate that when there is a will to change, change can happen [amplification].'

If you were using PowerPoint, you would have just one slide for this First Tell-um and it would look something like this:

Global Warming
– the greatest threat

- *Kyoto Accord* – global action
- *Local Authority waste management* – local action

Second Tell-um – Tell what you are going to tell them

The Second Tell-um is the body of your presentation. It is where you explore in depth the arguments you are making – delivering your messages and substantiating them with evidence, history and third party endorsement.

Third Tell-um – Tell them what you have just told them

With your Third Tell-um, you remind the audience of your key points. You summarise your arguments. You may well use that first overhead again.

Don't tail off at that point. Have a strong closing statement prepared, which contains your main message and sends the audience off on a high. (See Chapter 5 – Strong Closings.)

Memorable structures

The Three Tell-um structure is a sound one. It can be adapted to make your messages more memorable.

(i) Reduce each of your key messages to one word and make an *acronym* of the first letter of each of the words

Or

(ii) Reduce each of your key messages to one word and ensure that there is a *conceptual link* between the words or a *metaphor* capable of linking the words.

Structure your presentation around your messages

Your messages are the key building blocks around which you structure your presentation.

Each message should have its own section of the presentation.

Example

Developing a memorable structure for a presentation on strategic planning

Your presentation is to be about the process of strategic planning. You want to explain that there are four phases of the process:

- Review where you are at present
- Determine your aims and objectives and action points
- Implement the strategy
- Monitor and evaluate progress

Reducing this to four key words, we get – 'review', 'plan', 'implement', 'evaluate'

Acronyms

If you decide to go down the acronym route you need to find four other words, which mean the same, but give you an acronym, which itself sums up your message. How about POEM – a poem of praise for good management:

Preparation [Review]

Objectives [Plan]

Effort or Execution [Implement]

Monitoring [Evaluate]

Or maybe four words beginning with the same letter – the Four Es:

Examine

Establish aims

Execute

Evaluate

Conceptual link/metaphor

Find a *concept* for linking your four key words, e.g. a journey:

[Review] Where are we now? Get out the map, and locate where we are now

[Plan] Where do we want to go – find the destination and plot the route

[Implement] Driving there

[Evaluate] Looking at the holiday snaps afterwards

Other ideas that might fit are baking a cake, making a pot of tea, or traffic lights:

Red – Stop and reflect

Amber – Get ready to go

Green – Go

Silver – Check your mirror

Signposts

Your structure should always be very clearly signposted. Never assume your audience can follow the complexities of your argument – ensure they are, at all times, crystal clear about where you are, and where you are going with your arguments.

A presentation is a real time, verbal communication. Your audience cannot freeze frame and go back to revisit something you have said. They cannot go back to the beginning as they might in a newspaper article. They need you to give them a sense of direction.

Signposts can be verbal or written.

Verbal signposts

Tell your audience where you are now and where you are going. Use emphasis on key words

> 'So, having looked at the *reasons* for the fall in the price of coffee, let's *now* look at the *devastating impact* it will have on the local people.'

Written signposts

Your overheads can act as signposts. Make sure they are short and clear and capable of helping the audience to concentrate on where you are now (long sentences on overheads will only confuse – aim for bullet points with just one or two words beside them).

Outline structure for a really good presentation

1. A few words of welcome, introduction etc. + brief statement of the purpose/aim of your presentation
2. Attention grabbing opening (e.g. a quote, a joke, a story, a question, a prop) which contains within it your main message
3. Outline your three key messages
4. Take the audience through your three key messages, one at a time, backing up each message with all the relevant facts, background, examples and quotes from others
5. Summarise, restating your three key messages
6. Give a strong closing statement, which clarifies what you want the audience to do and sends them off inspired

4
Attention grabbing openings

You have a couple of minutes to establish your credibility, to set the tone of your presentation. A well prepared, powerful opening is the best way to start – it grabs the audience and it sets the scene.

Don't forget that HOW you are seen is as important as WHAT you say. The 'set piece' opener comes after your 'entrance'. It must be accompanied by appropriate body language. Stand up slowly and gracefully. Stride to the lectern (where appropriate). Pause, look round at your audience. Smile. Then start.

Here are some possible ways of opening:

Quote

A quote can provide a strong, powerful opening if read, or recited with a bit of drama, good pauses etc. Short quotes can be put up on the screen and read, pause, then read again.

The quote should be long enough to be a quote (rather than a soundbite – probably more than one line) but not so long that it gets boring.

Try the following:

- A quote from a guru in your field (e.g. in the Hospice movement, a quote from Dame Cicely Saunders, who founded the Hospice movement, is always good value)
- A quote from another field, but with resonance for your talk (e.g. a Shakespeare speech, a poem)
- A quote from a customer or stakeholder (e.g. a letter from a customer; some statements that have been recorded at a customer consultation)
- A quote from a relevant report, diary, or other related written material (e.g. an Amnesty International spokesperson on China used a quote from the diary of a mother who lost her son in Tiananmen Square; a housing expert quoted from a government White Paper on supporting people)

Joke

A joke is often regarded as the classic opener for a presentation, but beware – jokes can be high risk. Make sure your joke cannot be seen as sexist, racist, irrelevant or trivialising. Unless you are very good at telling jokes, and unless you are absolutely sure that the joke will be enjoyed and understood by everyone present, don't do it!

However, if you feel that a joke is necessary for the occasion (e.g. a prize giving, an after dinner speech, a motivating session) you might be able to find what you are looking for on a joke website (try <www.mit.edu/people/jcb/jokes> for music jokes or <www.workjoke.com/projoke.htm> for jokes about different jobs).

Adding touches of humour to your presentation throughout is usually a better strategy than a full-on joke at the beginning!

Props 1- *real props*

All of us enjoy show and tell. Having some real props can make a talk come alive. Props can also provide the audience with an opportunity for using other senses – not just their ears to hear the presentation. They can see and touch them, too. (See Chapter 9 – Visual Aids.)

Props 2 – *symbols and metaphors*

You can use practically anything to symbolise your main message. Look around the room you are sitting in at this moment – choose an object at random. Now try to work out how you could use it to introduce your talk. Here is a real life example:

> *A mirror* – at a small workshop of ten people, a representative of an HIV/AIDS organisation walked round the group getting each participant to look into the mirror. When she had gone round everyone she paused and said, 'You've just done something that people with a new HIV/AIDS diagnosis sometimes find very hard to do – look in the mirror – because they feel they don't know who they are any more.'

For more examples see Chapter 9 – Visual Aids.

Picture/video/sound tape

Picture

They say a picture is worth a thousand words. Choose a strong photograph, or a painting – copy it onto PowerPoint, or take a large version with you (or, in a smaller group, pass it round). Show it, look at it yourself, take your time. Talk your audience through it.

> A senior nurse manager in a hospice was training nurses. She wanted to make the point that the patients themselves can contribute to each other's well-being, it is not all down to nurses. She put up a slide of a photograph of several elderly gents all having a good laugh wearing knitted hats in different colours. She explained that the men were all outpatients at the hospice, all were terminally ill (and had all since died), but they had had great fun as 'the hospice gnomes' after they had all been knitted these colourful pointed woolly caps by some of the ladies who came in for day treatment, too.

Video

A short video can transport your audience to another place, get them to see and hear something real. Don't use a video for the sake of it, it must earn its place in your presentation, i.e. it should help you meet your aims.

Sound tape

A sound tape can:

- play music – to change the mood in the room, or to energise your audience
- relay voices from elsewhere (e.g. people you have interviewed in the course of some research). It is sometimes difficult to hear disembodied voices clearly if you are sitting in a meeting so make sure the quality of the tape is good, the speakers are speaking slowly enough to be understood and the tape must be long enough for people to 'tune in' to the voices
- play sounds from elsewhere e.g. a whale, a nightingale, a siren, a crowd

Don't forget, the sound tape must always help you achieve your aims.

Party, party

Everyone enjoys the speaker who creates a party atmosphere and draws the audience into active participation. Being a showman/woman requires confidence and flair and can reap huge rewards. For example:

> The chief executive of a hospital trust had been asked to speak about SWOT analysis at a conference. He bounded onto the stage and called out to the audience, 'Who knows what the S in SWOT stands for?' Someone called out 'Strengths.' The speaker grinned, clapped and dug his hand in his pocket, pulling out a Mars bar which he chucked to the respondent, 'Well done, here is your prize. Now, who knows what the W stands for?' [It is a good idea to have a plant in the audience to ensure someone calls out the first answer!]
>
> A playworker was to give a presentation about the way children learn through play. He called up a couple of volunteers onto the

> stage and gave them a ball, asking them to throw it backwards and forwards to each other. He walked round them talking about the range of things a game of ball could teach [e.g. hand–eye coordination, cooperation, speed and velocity, arcs and parabolas].

Visualisation

If you want to draw your audience into your talk from the beginning, get them to shut their eyes (or not) and take them through a visualisation. Give very clear instructions (Now close your eyes. I want you to think about... Can you see...?)

> A housing services manager was opening a speech to tenants in which he was going to have to argue for higher rents in return for better housing services. He asked his audience to visualise their blocks of flats. He was going to take them on a guided tour without leaving the meeting hall. 'Let's go in, through the double doors, they are looking rather battered aren't they, and one of the panes of glass is cracked. I'll hold the door open for you... I'm afraid it's very dingy inside, isn't it? There is no light, because the bulb is broken, and the walls are covered in graffiti. It is rather grimy and uninviting, and down there, behind the stairs there is rubbish... We all know this is not acceptable. Year after year we have kept the rents down, and that has put a squeeze on services, we have got to put rents up if we are to provide a decent environment.'

Question

A challenging, open question (who, what, why, where, when, how) can make a powerful opener. Give the audience time to respond. Don't rush on. Wait for a reply (again, you might need a plant to give you confidence that someone will respond). Acknowledge all replies positively, this will get the audience on your side, because you are listening to them. In a smaller workshop setting, you might want to consider writing up the answers on a flip chart.

Don't ask closed questions to which there is a right answer (e.g., What is the population of the UK?) – people are reluctant to answer questions they may get wrong.

Statistic

Do you have a killer statistic that sums up your message? That will shock, entertain, or concentrate the minds of your audience? If you do, you might want to use it for your opener. The trick with using a statistic in this way is to play it for all it is worth. Don't say it once and rush on to the First Tell-um. The audience will lose the significance – they may not even hear it (remember this is your opener, they are just getting used to the sound of your voice). You have got to ham it up a bit.

Say the statistic. Put it up on a PowerPoint slide. Repeat it (maybe expressed in a slightly different way (e.g. 53% – over half)). Ask the audience if they realised this fact. Talk a bit about the significance of the statistic. Say it again.

Example
'25% of children under ten living in the UK live below the poverty line. 25%. A quarter of children living in families who are below the poverty line. Parents who can't afford expensive trainers, who can't afford holidays, who worry about where every penny is coming from. One in every four children lives like that in Britain. Now. Today.'

5
Strong closings

It is important to send your audience off feeling good about themselves, about you and about your message. Don't let your presentation stutter to a halt. Build up to a crescendo! Ensure that this is a memorable experience – not just another boring talk.

After your Third Tell-um (the summary), pause and deliver your strong closing remarks.

Use words that signal the close, and increase concentration:

'And Finally...'

'Just one last word before I finish...'

'So, there is one last thought I'd like to send you off with...'

Then go on to the strong close. Examples of closings with impact are:

- A short quote which summarises your main message (e.g. the warm words of a satisfied customer, a poem with a strong rhythm)
- A couple of paragraphs with a good soundbite at their heart (see Chapter 2)
- Re-iterating a key aspect of your attention grabbing opening

After delivering your strong close, pause, look round at your audience, then walk smoothly back to your seat.

6
Handling questions

A presentation should not just be a one way communication. It should normally be the prelude to a two way dialogue – questions and answers.

Decide whether you are prepared to take questions as you go through your talk. If you decide you would rather handle questions at the end, make this clear to the audience.

Either:

'Do chip in and ask me questions as we go.'

Or:

'My presentation is about 15 minutes long, I'll be happy to take questions afterwards.'

Anticipate questions

Your preparation should include anticipating questions. That way you should be able to answer most of them in the presentation itself. Preparation also enables you to be prepared for difficult or hostile questions.

Handling questions

Respond to questions with your conclusion (the gist of your answer) first – then explain why you have reached that conclusion (providing facts, anecdotes etc.). Don't give lots of information, building up to the conclusion because you will lose your audience.

Responding to questions to which you do not know the answer

Don't:

- Lie or make something up
- Waffle
- Present yourself as someone who doesn't know the answer (that can undermine your authority)

Do:

- Present yourself as someone who cares about accuracy, 'I'm afraid I don't know the precise answer to that, and I really don't want to give you the wrong information... I will find out and get back to you.'

Handling hostile questions

Don't:

- Get angry – meeting hostility with hostility

Do:

- Try to understand why people are angry or hostile (allow yourself to imagine what the world looks like to them – you don't have to say you agree with them or anything like that, but, inside your head try to see them as distressed rather than a pain in the neck)
- Maintain a reasonable, open tone
- Go through a three part answer:
  - Empathise (this is not the same as agreeing) – 'I understand that you must be angry'
  - Restate your position
  - Ask if that answers their point
- Agree to talk to them afterwards

The objection

Sometimes you will be met with a head-on objection ('This is all nonsense!'), sometimes it will be a hidden objection ('Why are the charges so high?'). Don't get defensive. Give a four part reply:

- Clarify the precise objection ('So you feel...')
- Provide context and perspective ('As you know, we have held our charges for the past three years...')
- Restate your original position
- Mention the benefits of your position ('This will enable us to improve the service in the following ways...')

The show-off

A question will often be more about demonstrating the questioner's knowledge and skill than about eliciting information from you – they may be showing off to you or to their colleagues. They will be pleased if you flatter them ('Of course, you are dead right – this is a very specialised technical area, I am not completely convinced it will make much difference, but I am glad you raised it').

The irrelevant question

Sometimes you get asked a question that suggests the questioner has not really been listening. This is the time to use the bridging technique.

- Acknowledge the question (e.g. 'I know some people take that view...'; 'I understand where you are coming from...')
- Bridge ('...but let's look at it from another angle...'; '...but the research suggests a rather different picture...')
- Talk about a more relevant or important issue

The test question

This is the type of question you may get asked in a competitive bid presentation. The question that is attempting to probe the extent of your knowledge and experience. Never try to bluff. If you know the answer, give it. If you don't know the answer turn yourself from someone who doesn't know into someone who cares about accuracy ('I'm sorry, I'm afraid I really don't know the answer to that, and I certainly wouldn't want to give you the wrong answer, But I know a man who does, and I'll get back to you tomorrow').

7
You – personal presence and body language

A compelling personal presence is very valuable for anyone whose work involves giving presentations or meeting people. It is sometimes called charisma. It helps you make real contact with your audience, and leaves a lasting impression.

Although some people naturally seem to have a powerful presence, much of it can be learned.

You can develop your personal presence by working on:

(i) *How you present yourself*
(ii) *Understanding how your audience thinks*

How you present yourself

1. Your inner sense of self

Confidence

Don't forget that people take you at your own evaluation of yourself – so it is important to appear confident. Your nerves are your responsibility, not your audience's.

Confident people:

- Maintain eye contact
- Speak so that everyone can hear
- Fill the space around them
- Appear relaxed
- Engage/communicate with the audience rather than with themselves
- Appear to know what is expected of them

- Are generous, they are not self absorbed – they refer to other people's concerns/what other people have said/to other people present
- Are relatively informal when giving a presentation (unless it is a very formal occasion)

How to be more confident:

- Prepare well
- Don't worry too much about nerves – they are never as noticeable to your audience as they are to you. Adrenalin gives you an edge which makes your presentation more affecting
- Think 'I'm not nervous, I'm excited!'

Recognising confidence

Question

Think about a confident person whose presenting style you admire. Write down three physical manifestations of their confidence – why do you assume they are confident, what are they doing that gives them an aura of confidence?

Visualisation to help you think big and confident

Close your eyes, you are going to think big – make yourself big, make your voice big, make your personality big.

Imagine you are in a room where you are to give a presentation. See yourself stride confidently across the platform, or across the space. Take large strides. Slow down. Take your strides, confidently and slowly. Feel good about taking these confident, slow strides. It is your space. Walk to the front of the stage.

Pause, look around, smile. Look at the audience. Help them feel good about themselves as you look at them.

Now you start your presentation. Say how glad you are to be there. Thank the audience for inviting you. Look round at them. Smile again. You mean it. This is going to be a good event, and it is because you are their speaker.

Use power words to focus your energy

How would you like to come over? What impression would you like to create? How do you want your audience to think about you? Tough and dynamic, perhaps. Or maybe warm and friendly. Perhaps you'd prefer inspiring and enthusiastic. How about calm and authoritative?

It helps to name how you want to come across. It can help you focus your energy and centre yourself. It can get you into the right frame of mind to make a stunning presentation.

Athletes often use this technique to prepare themselves before a race (they use words like *excellence* and *winning*). They concentrate hard, using their power words to focus on how it feels, looks and sounds to be excellent and a winner.

Choose words that are realistic, but aspirational – *you*, as you would like to be seen. *You* as a worthy representative of your organisation. Look at the list of words below. Choose a couple that really do the business for you. If you can't see a word you want on the list – just add it in. These are *your* words.

Some suggested words (but you may prefer others)

Affable	Angry	Businesslike	Bold	Creative	Candid
Approachable	Commanding	Comfortable	Challenging	Canny	Calm
Direct	Dynamic	Daring	Dashing	Engaging	Empathetic
Energetic	Electrifying	Flirtatious	Formidable	Forceful	Gracious
Genial	Glamorous	Gutsy	Hearty	Happy	Inspiring
Innovative	Impressive	Influential	Jovial	Jaunty	Kind
Lively	Responsive	Provocative	Powerful	Passionate	Spirited
Suave	Sassy	Tough	Trustworthy	Vigorous	Wise
Warm	Friendly	Modern	Elegant	Plain speaking	Vibrant

Being centred

Being centred, focused, ready to engage, is an important part of personal presence. It is both a physical and a psychological state.

- Physically it is about being relaxed, but energised
- Psychologically it is about feeling strong, confident, mentally alert and ready. Give yourself time

Generosity to others

- Generosity facilitates communication – it helps you touch your audience. Charismatic speakers tend to be generous, not self absorbed, they think about their audience. The audience feels validated by the speaker's generosity

Think positive

It is important to think positively about yourself. If you don't rate yourself, the audience won't either.

- Tell yourself you feel confident and compelling
- Look in the mirror, look yourself straight in the eyes and say, 'You're good', 'You're a strong presenter', 'You've got what it takes'
- Hear yourself, hear the strength in your voice as you say – 'Yes, I'm good'
- Smile at yourself

Talk positive

Reinforce your positive thinking whenever you can. For example, if someone asks you how you feel before you are due to give a speech...

Don't say:
'I'm really worried about it.'

Do say something like:
'It'll be a challenge, but I'm looking forward to it.'

By responding positively you are supporting your own positive image of yourself, and projecting a confident and professional image to others.

This is not the same as boasting or being arrogant. Boastfulness is often a sign of lack of confidence and it is not generous to others.

Self awareness

It is not just your presentation and the words you use that send messages to your audience. Be aware of how others will 'read you' – avoid being stereotyped, think of your audience, 'match' them.

Be aware of:

- How you walk into a room – try to be relaxed and confident from the moment you arrive

- What you wear
- How you listen
- How you relate to your fellow speakers

The more confident you appear, the more power your message will have.

2. Creating a good impression

Impression management

Creating a good impression requires 'impression management'.

Give a good impression from the moment you arrive (and even before, by being professional and efficient about arrangements).

As a presenter, there are two key stages in impression management:

- When you first arrive at the venue
- When you are giving your presentation

How to create a good impression when you first arrive at the venue

How you look

Your clothes: Dress to match your audience (or slightly smarter). Remember that when you arrive, your overcoat may create the first impression.

Your hair: Smart and professional. Brushed.

Carrying your materials etc. Look neat and professional. Carry your materials in a neat and coordinated way (i.e. one good-quality brief case, not lots of bags and rolls of paper and files and parcels).

Your body language – open and purposeful.

What you say

As you arrive, you are creating a powerful impression. You need to see this period as the prelude to your presentation. So...

Don't say (even as a joke):

- 'I'm nervous'
- I'd like to get this over with as soon as possible'

Do:

- Express interest in the event
- Ask about the audience
- Clarify technical issues (e.g. check equipment is working)
- Clarify any contextual issues (e.g. who else is going to be speaking, though you should ideally have done that before; whether there have been any changes in circumstances)

What you do

When you meet people on your arrival pay close attention to your body language – open hand gestures, grounded with your feet, head high, good eye contact (remember ordinary conversational eye contact is about 60% – in this greeting phase aim for about 70%).

How to create a good impression when you are giving your presentation

You have a short time to make a first impression on your audience.

How do you want them to feel? What do you want them to see? What do you want them to think? What do you want them to hear?

When you get up to speak... Draw all eyes to you.

- Think about how you are occupying the space around you, make the space your own
- Think about your posture – stand tall, walk tall, take your time
- Focus yourself, using your power words
- Use pauses and eye contact to 'touch' your audience
- Memorise your first two sentences. Say them in an upbeat way

3. How you occupy space

While you are speaking, the space (if you are on a stage, the whole stage) is yours. Take possession of it.

Being grounded/taking the floor

If possible, always visit the venue beforehand and think about the layout and how it will affect how you use the space. If a visit is impossible, spend a few minutes, when you first arrive, deciding how to use the space.

Issues to consider:

- Will you stand or sit?
- Where will you stand or sit?
- If there is a lectern will you need to use it, or will you come out from behind it?
- Will you remain static, or will you walk?
- Will you stay 'on stage' or will you walk around your audience?
- What implication for your visual aids will these decisions have?

Moving

Some of the most experienced speakers move, with purpose, around the stage. They move towards their audience. They talk directly to sections of their audience (while not ignoring the rest of the audience). It certainly gives out confident and 'experienced' signals.

Do:

- Move slowly and deliberately, pausing to reground yourself
- Use your new position to look with renewed interest at this section of your audience
- Think about how far to move (just on the stage, around the room etc.)
- Think about the combination of movement and your use of visual aids

Don't:

- Jiggle on the spot
- Sway
- Pace backwards and forwards
- Move out of the light (e.g. if there is a spotlight)
- Move out of the range of the audio system

Making the stage/space your own

You can occupy the space of the stage, not just by walking/sitting etc., but also by redefining or claiming the space.

Redefining and claiming the space:

- Come out from behind the lectern
- Push the table back
- Erect a 'display', e.g. a map, a poster related to your speech, which will be on view the whole time
- Make sure other people's flip charts and equipment are removed
- Take your jacket off (if the setting is relatively informal) and put it over the back of the chair
- Put up a slide with your name and title on it

Don't:

Spread messy slides, notes and other paraphernalia around – it looks very unprofessional

Spatial positioning

Be aware that your spatial positioning in relationship to your audience (high/low; near/far; right/left) will have an impact on how you are understood.

There is no absolute right or wrong in spatial positioning, just things to bear in mind.

High/low

If you are higher than your audience, it usually implies power and authority, but it can be read as arrogance or domination. So you would probably want to be up on a stage for a new product launch, but on the flat if announcing redundancies.

You can deliberately reject a given spatial relationship and 'claim' the space as your own; e.g., one speaker deliberately chose to get down off the stage and give his talk from the aisle and the area in front of the stage. He used a clip-on mike.

Near/far

Even if you are speaking in a huge auditorium, your aim is to make every person in the audience feel you are speaking to them, that they have some relationship to you. You have to bridge the distance. Do this by walking up to the edge of the stage, slowly scan the audience throughout your presentation.

Right/left

Some settings are biased to right or left – a lectern is placed to one side of the stage, the lighting privileges one side of the stage, most of the audience seems to be sitting over to one side of the room etc. If there is nothing you can do about this, make sure your eye contact is inclusive and takes in the whole audience.

You also need to be aware of any tendency you may have to look more in one direction or the other. Be aware, too, that a dominant person (e.g. a VIP, the person who asks most questions, or just the most startlingly beautiful person) can make you look towards their side of the room. Maintain inclusive eye contact with all members of the audience at all times.

Drawing all eyes to you at the beginning of your speech

When you get up to speak draw all eyes to you by ...

- Pausing
- Focusing
- Looking at the audience – left, centre, right
- Smiling

4. Non-verbal communication

Language came fairly late on in human development. So it is hardly surprising that human beings can be very sophisticated communicators without words. We can tell if someone is smiling even if we cannot see them.

As Desmond Morris says,

> 'Frequently the human animal... concentrates so hard on his words that he seems to forget that his movements, postures and expressions are telling their own story.'

A study by US psychologist Mehrabian suggested that only 7% of the information we take in when a person is speaking is verbal. The remaining 93% is non-verbal. Over half (55%) of our impact is visual – posture and body language, facial expressions, what we are wearing etc., and 37% is vocal including tone, pitch, volume, inflection and pace. Only about 7% of what we experience when a person is talking is the content of the words.

You are 'selling' *yourself* every bit as much as you are selling your organisation, your ideas or product.

Make your non-verbal communication work for you.

Non-verbal communication:

- Body language
- Facial expressions
- Clothes
- Personality
- Voice – pitch, tone etc.

Body language

Body language is about *all* the communicating you are doing with your body. All your body language is a form of communication with the audience. It includes:

- How you stand
- How you sit
- What you do with your hands
- What you do with your feet

Body language is so important, that you must get it right. This is an area in which it can be very useful indeed to have some one-to-one coaching support, or practice with a video camera (much better than practising in front of the mirror).

Use your body as a powerful communication tool. Probably the most important thing is to ensure your body language is open.

Hands and arms

Use your hands with ease. Develop gestures that are natural, expressive and purposeful. The right gestures can help you convey your message, they add animation. But they can be distracting if overused.

Gestures work best when they help illustrate a point you are making. By getting your body involved, you have a better chance of involving the audience.

The more space you are willing to use, the more power you communicate.

Exercise

Get outside your comfort zone with your gestures. Make big gestures. Make slow gestures. Make descriptive gestures.

Describe the following using just hand gestures and facial expressions:

- A great opportunity
- A four point plan
- A new initiative
- A choppy time ahead
- A world beater

Do:

- Anchor your hands by lightly clasping them in front of you, elbows away from your body. Then move out from there with occasional hand gestures
- Use hand gestures to emphasise a point

- Make hand (and body) gestures which reflect what you are saying (e.g. 'All around the world…'). Don't do them apologetically – make them big, make them work for you
- Use your hands to add punctuation
- Use open hand gestures, palms upwards
- Get some coaching help with hand gestures, or practice yourself with a video camera

Don't:

- Berate with a wagging finger
- Point with a jabbing motion
- Fiddle with bits of clothing or your hair
- Wave your hands around like windmills

Minimising your hand gestures

If you feel you overuse your hands:

Do:

- Anchor your hands with a pen or pointer, or
- Anchor your hands by lightly clasping them in front of you, holding them low. Occasionally varying this by moving your hands to waist height and putting fingertips together, fingers spread
- Hold small cards with notes
- Lightly rest your hands on a lectern or the back of a chair

Don't:

- Put your hands in your pockets
- Fold your arms
- Grip the lectern
- Anchor your hands with a pen but then keep clicking it, or taking the top on and off
- Hold a scrap of paper (it looks untidy, and you might start folding it)

Your head

Try to become aware of how you hold your head, how you move your head.

- Your head slightly down, and on one side, looks docile and weak
- Your head up, standing tall, looks professional and confident
- Use your head expressively, to accompany facial gestures
- Make sure your hair is well cut and brushed. A fringe should be short and neat (not in your eyes – otherwise you will be peering out from underneath it). Women's long hair is best worn up (you want an uncluttered silhouette)

Feet and legs

You need to be balanced, grounded, centred.

Do:

- Place feet parallel, pointed forward and about six to eight inches apart.
- Distribute your weight evenly between both feet.
- Feel like a tree, with your roots going down into the ground, claiming the space, holding you secure
- Hold your body evenly balanced, feel well grounded, breathe deeply

Don't:

- Rest on one leg, with hip jutted out – it looks like a slouch
- Wrap your legs round one another – this is closed body language
- Have your legs too far apart – it looks belligerent
- Tap your foot
- Jig from one foot to the other

Walking onto the stage with confidence

Do:

- Stride with energy and vigour
- Have a spring in your step
- Hold your head high
- Know what route across the stage you will take, don't trip over

Don't:

- Walk too fast, remember to be composed and authoritative
- Shuffle
- Use small, timid movements, they undermine your authority

Posture: standing

Your posture shows people how you feel about yourself and how you feel about walking into a room or giving a presentation.

A hunched posture communicates insecurity, tiredness or lack of energy. A rigid posture can communicate inflexibility and arrogance.

Be grounded and relaxed. This communicates strength and commitment. Develop a stance that reaches out, communicating enthusiasm and openness.

Standing is the natural position for a speaker because it conveys authority and confidence.

Do:

- Straighten your spine
- Hold your head high
- Keep your shoulders down
- Relax your neck and shoulder muscles
- Hold your stomach in
- Place your feet six to eight inches apart, and balance weight evenly between them

Exercise

Imagine a string attached to the top of your head, pulling you up. Pause. Look round, smile.

Don't:

- Wrap yourself up in closed body language
- Look at your feet – it looks as if you can't face your audience
- Tilt your head back and jut out your jaw – it looks aggressive and arrogant
- Hold your head on one side – it looks weak or patronising

Posture: sitting

Even if you get to your feet to speak, you will probably be sitting down for most of the event. How you sit conveys messages about you to your audience.

Don't forget that you are 'on show' all the time. How you sit is important.

Do:

- Sit upright
- Sit well back in your seat – supported by the chair back
- Be alert, be present, interested in what is going on (not day-dreaming or preoccupied)

Don't:

- Slouch or slide down in your chair
- Lean on one arm of the chair
- Put your arm along the back of your neighbour's chair
- Go to sleep (or even close your eyes)
- Leaf through papers, or lean over and start searching your briefcase

5. Facial expressions

Being open

Your face is an important communicator – perhaps *the* most important. Your audience will focus on your face, and will read your expressions. They will look at your face, and decide whether or not they can trust you. An open face, genuine smile and a sparkle in the eyes will immediately open the doors to greater rapport with your audience. Imagine your face saying 'Yes!'

Your audience will 'pick up' whether your smile is genuine or false, they will know if you are bored or angry – even if you are trying to cover it up. So get yourself into the right frame of mind before you speak.

Be as open as you can. Your face will signal this through:

- Good eye contact
- Widening your eyes from time to time (your eyebrows are very powerful at sending messages)
- Not frowning
- Not looking down at your feet

Be positive and energetic

Tiredness, lack of concentration, preoccupation with something else – all this shows in your face and will act as a barrier to communication.

Be positive. Look healthy and energetic (do you need make-up?).

The language of facial expressions

Some facial expressions have a universal meaning – especially:

- Smiling
- Frowning

6. Voice

Using your voice to optimum effect

Your voice – its tone, pitch, clarity – can draw people towards you. Your voice can influence, motivate, relax, energise. It can help people decide whether or not they respect you, relate to you or believe you.

In order to use your voice to optimum effect think about:

- Projection
- The range and variety of your voice
- Breathing
- Pitch
- Tone
- Pace
- Clarity

Voice Projection

Instead of forcing the sound with muscles, it is more effective to focus on getting the air flow moving.

Exercises

Some exercises to get the air flow moving:

Hey

Say 'Hey' in a loud voice. Then stop at the end of the word, and be conscious of your abdominal muscles being tight.

Hold a hand out in front of your mouth (start at four inches or so then move out). Feel the air as you say 'Hey'. In order to make the voice travel farther, you need to increase the air flow.

Move your hands out to about ten to twelve inches, aim the air farther. Then imagine the air travelling to the back of the room. Have the air do the work instead of your throat muscles.

Poem

Lie on your back with your knees slightly bent. Read a poem (or rehearse your presentation). If you're lying down, it is difficult to breathe wrongly.

Variety

We've all listened to boring, monotonous presenters. Variety of pace, pitch, emphasis etc. is vital to retain your audience's concentration and interest. Think of your voice as an orchestra – you have a wide range of sounds, tones and pitches available to you.

Exercises

You have a wider repertoire than you thought you had, reprogramme yourself:

- Explore how it feels to say words very slooooooowly…then very quickly
- Practise saying words loudly, as well as very softly
- Practise reading a short piece from the newspaper 'in the manner of the word', i.e. happily, or boldly, or challengingly, or enthusiastically or inspiringly
- Be aware of rhythm – some passages of your presentation will benefit from rhythmical phrasing (try reading some of those old Victorian recitation poems by Tennyson or Wordsworth)

Breathing

Speaking in public, giving presentations, is known to be one of people's greatest fears – and fear can inhibit good breathing. Sometimes you can almost forget to breathe!

When you are nervous, your breathing tends to be shallow. You use just your upper chest muscles rather than your diaphragm and abdominal muscles. This makes your voice weaker and you will look and sound less confident.

So, take your time. Breathe. Breathe deeply. Breathe rhythmically. Control your breathing. Slow it right down, count as you breathe in, count as you breathe out.

Full breathing helps your voice become more resonant, your mind becomes clearer, and your gestures appear more natural.

7. Mannerisms

Recognising your mannerisms

It is important to recognise your mannerisms and to decide whether they are good or bad (get someone else to help you do this).

You can undo bad mannerisms and learn good habits, but it takes time. There is a ladder of learning that has to be gone through.

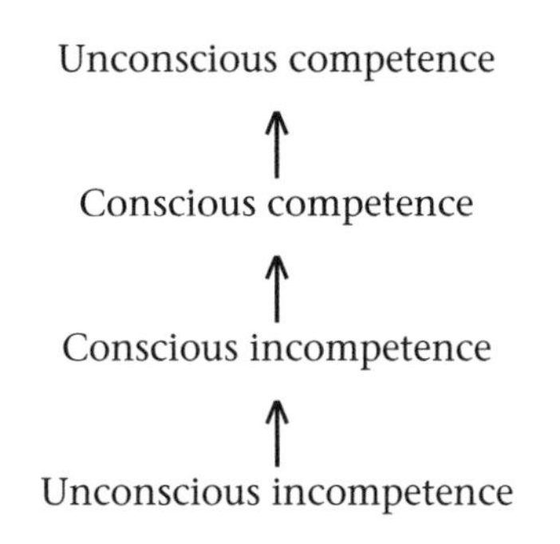

Take, for example, saying 'um' a lot. Learn to pause rather than say 'um'.

You need, first of all, to realise you are saying 'um' a lot. Then you have to become consciously competent for six weeks (i.e. all the time you are speaking, to friends, at meetings, at home, at work you must consciously pause rather than say 'um'). After six weeks you will pause quite naturally.

Resisting stereotyping

The audience will 'read' what you say in the light of how they perceive you. Make sure their perceptions are the ones you want. Avoid being stereotyped.

Stereotypes are very powerful. If your audience can stereotype you, they probably will. This will put you in a box, from which it will be very difficult to break free (you can sometimes use stereotyping to your advantage, of course).

What negative stereotyping would you want to avoid?

To avoid being stereotyped

- Be self aware, assess honestly whether you could be easily stereotyped and act to get out of your box!
- Match your audience

Matching is not the same as mirroring or imitating (that can be insulting and very off putting). Matching is a natural response. People having a friendly conversation tend to match each other's gestures – when one leans back the other will too. When one picks up a cup to drink, her friend probably will as well.

Matching the gestures of another person helps them identify with you.

If you are giving a presentation to a small group (especially if it is one to one), match gestures, maintain eye contact. Look for signs that the audience are matching your gestures (this is an encouraging sign).

Matching language

Most people naturally make slight modifications to their voice and language in order to be 'in tune' with their audience. But always be yourself and watch out for jargon (even if the audience use lots of jargon, don't slavishly follow their lead!).

The following extract from the *Guardian* newspaper (London, 19 May 2001) demonstrates how far politicians go to reflect the style of their audience:

> A colleague kindly points out to me that there are sets of headphones available, and that if I put one on I will be able to hear what Tony Blair says to the [police] recruits. I put on the headphones, which I imagine, at first, are not working. Then I realise that they are indeed working and that what I am hearing

is the prime minister. He is saying such things as "Yeah, whur, aarh, shrdlu, shrdlu, shrdlu". He is running through a kind of muscle memory in his vocal chords, in order to produce an accent which will approximate to that of the recruit. This is something that I have heard about and seen demonstrated on television, this is 'accommodation' in his speech patterns. But this is the first time I have followed the prime minister and seen how often he does it. I sympathise, because although it is largely an attempt at mateyness, it is also a form of awkward politeness.

8. Handling your nervousness

There are two aspects of being nervous – physical and mental.

Physical

Try one or more of the following physical relaxation exercises:

- Take deep breaths. Count up to five slowly as you breathe in, then count up to five slowly as you breathe out
- Get endorphins whizzing round your body by tightening all your muscles (work up from your toes, tightening every muscle). Once you have tightened all your muscles, hold it for a few seconds, then take a deep breath in – as you exhale relax all your muscles together
- Relax your shoulders, relax your neck muscles, turn your head one way, then the other

Mental

1. *Don't worry too much about being nervous*

   Nerves can give you an edge. Some of the most professional and experienced speakers still get nervous – they often say it helps them keep on their toes!

   Also, we can't see inside your head where all the nervous thoughts are jangling. You almost never seem as nervous as you feel.

2. *Reframe your nerves*

   Don't think about that feeling as nervousness, think about it as excitement. It is the same chemical going round your system – adrenalin.

3. *Think positive*

   Use your focus words to help you get your head in the right place.

A quick guide to style!

(with thanks to Style Counsel)

Looking good has seven component parts:

- Shape of your body – your bodyline
- Shape of your face
- Scale
- Colour
- Appropriate for the occasion
- Currency – needs to be modern
- Reflecting your 'fashion personality'

Bodyline

Bodyline is probably the most important of the seven components.

Women's bodylines

Straight (e.g. Princess Diana)

- Little or no waist emphasis
- Straight, long ribcage
- Flat hips
- Flat thighs

If your bodyline is straight, you will look best in straight, tailored garments with little waist emphasis.

Tapered

- Short ribcage/low bust (small gap between bust and waist)
- Visible waistline
- Rounded hips/thighs
- Hips appear high

Should go for 'fit and flair', avoid belts and tucked in shirts.

Curved (e.g. Marilyn Monroe)

- Long ribcage/high bust
- Obvious waistline
- Low hips
- Flared hips/thighs

The main difference between this and the tapered figure is the longer ribcage and the higher bust. Can wear waisted clothes, floaty clothes because they are curvy and have movement.

Fuller

- Full bust
- Wide ribcage
- Little or no waist
- Full hips/thighs

Rectangular, like the straight bodyline, but bigger all over. Should wear straight clothes, with no waistline. Avoid details like pockets on the bustline.

Men's bodylines

Triangular

- Broad shoulders
- Small waist
- Narrow hips
- Tapered rib cage

Can wear tucked in tops, bomber jackets, wide lapels and double breasted.

Rectangular

- Shoulders, waist, hips all similar measurements
- Straight ribcage

Needs moderately padded shoulders, should wear longer casual jackets, straight legged trousers.

Contoured

- Narrow shoulders
- Fuller waist
- Rounded hips/tum
- Wide ribcage

Should wear substantial padding to build up shoulders, single breasted jackets and flat fronted trousers with straight leg.

Face shapes

Main shapes are:

Curved/rounded

- Oval – lucky you, you can wear most hairstyles
- Round
- Heart
- Pear

Straight/sharper

- Square
- Rectangle
- Diamond

Features – eyebrows, eyes, nose, mouth

- Rounded
- Straight

You need to decide whether your face + features are predominantly *straight* or predominantly *rounded*.

If you are predominantly 'rounded', go for slightly rounded or wavy hairstyles and rounded/oval glasses, earring shapes, necklace shapes etc.

If you are predominantly 'straight' you can wear sharper, more geometric hairstyles and glasses and accessories with straight lines.

Scale

You also need to consider *scale*. Are you:

- Large/tall/big boned?
- Medium build?
- Small/petite?

Wear accessories (e.g. earrings, necklaces, handbags) which mirror your scale. A tiny handbag looks wrong when carried by a tall, big boned woman.

Colour

Every colour has a number of properties:

- Depth – how deep or light it is
- Clarity – how clear or muted it is
- Undertone – whether it has blue or yellow undertones

In order to gauge the colours that suit you best, you need to consider your skin colouring, your eye colour and your hair colour to determine your own depth, clarity and undertone.

As a rule of thumb:

- Fair hair + light eyes = wear light colours
- Fair hair + dark eyes = wear muted colours
- Reddish hair + light eyes = wear warm colours
- Dark hair + dark eyes = wear deep colours
- Dark hair + light eyes = wear bright colours; high contrast
- Grey hair + pale skin + light eyes = wear cool colours

The colours you choose will be affected by your skin tone – someone with a yellow skin tone should go for colours with a yellow undertone, a blue skin tone means going towards colours with a blue undertone. Many colours (e.g. green, red, blue) have versions with a blue or yellow undertone – so don't think you can't wear green, you may just not have found the right green.

Appropriate dress

Clothes that are appropriate for your lifestyle and for the occasion

Everyone needs a flexible, versatile wardrobe which suits their lifestyle. The most useful wardrobe for a mum at home with kids will obviously not be the most useful for a businesswoman.

So decide what are the demands on your wardrobe. Also, go through your clothes and consider what are your most useful pieces.

The idea is to get a sensible 'cost per wear' (a cheap jacket you wear once is far more expensive than an expensive jacket you wear 300 times). Most people wear 20% of their clothes 80% of the time.

They also say you should 'dress for the job you want rather than the job you have'. Go for the best you can afford.

When you are deciding what to wear for a presentation – follow the dress code of the occasion.

Build a capsule wardrobe around your needs. A capsule wardrobe for a working woman consists of:

Core:

a pair of jeans

a white shirt

1 black dress

1 coat or rain coat

Basics:

2 pieces of knitwear

2 suits:

- a skirt
- a pair of trousers
- 2 jackets

3 tops

1 day dress

1 pair of trousers

1 two-piece dress

Remember the rule of three – everything should be able to be worn three ways.

Accessories:

Jewellery

Glasses

Shoes

Belts

Hosiery

Scarves and hats

Bags

Currency

Your clothes need to be reasonably current. This is very important. If you look old fashioned your views will also be seen as out of date.

It does not mean trendy or just off the catwalk (it is not about mutton dressing as lamb!) but it does mean wearing clothes and accessories that have a modern feel rather than being leftovers from a bygone era. Be particularly careful about this if you are someone who buys a lot from charity shops.

Real zeros are:

- Out of date glasses (even Coronation Street's Deirdre is wearing smaller glasses these days!)

- 80s highly padded shoulders and oversized fit (you may well want a bit of shoulder padding, but not the heavy padding of the 80s)
- Out of date colours (e.g. Thatcher blue – it is very 80s)
- Trousers too short
- Red braces
- Trousers with pleated fronts
- Out of date hairstyles (e.g. an 80s bob)
- Cardigans with pictures on
- Shoes – make sure your shoes are current, otherwise they are particularly ageing

Stereotyping

Beware clothes and accessories that stereotype you – long earrings for social workers, designer stubble for designers and film makers.

Your own fashion personality

People tend to be:

- Trendy (this is usually the young), or
- Contemporary (this is the best bet for women over 30), or
- Classic (very safe, old fashioned way of dressing – can be ageing)

But there are other subdivisions, too:

- Tailored (Armani)
- Romantic (Chloe)
- Zany (Versace, D&G)
- Glamorous (Alexander McQueen, Marc Jacobs)
- Intellectual (Prada)

Knowing your style, and developing a wardrobe that is coherent and appropriate for your lifestyle is key.

8
Building rapport with your audience

You audience's first moments' experience of you is crucial. If you are able to communicate trust, integrity and warmth in those first few seconds, you have gained an enormous advantage.

There is a primitive part of our brain that decides whether or not to trust. At the unconscious level we are attending to many non-verbal cues. Signals such as eye contact, posture, tone of voice and breathing will help determine whether or not we feel safe with someone (see Chapter 7).

There are other techniques, too, that can help you develop rapport with your audience. Many of them, described in this chapter, are based on NLP (Neuro-Linguistic Programming).

BUILDING RAPPORT

Barriers to communication

When looking at rapport, it is useful to understand what some of the barriers to communication are.

Your audience are not blank sheets of paper. They come with experience and knowledge. They also come with prejudices, expectations and preconceived notions – some of these will, of course, help you and make the audience predisposed to listen. Others present hurdles for you to overcome.

> You need to understand the source of some of this baggage. Baggage can include negative experience and perspectives on the subject, or about the organisation responsible for the event. They may feel negative about a woman/man/old/young etc. speaker. Some baggage may be current preoccupations (personal things going on in their own lives that make them edgy or bad tempered, or distant and unable to hear or to participate).

Don't take negativity personally. Be positive, be prepared.

Warm words

Warm words draw people towards you. Try to use warm words in your presentations. For example:

- Hope
- Trust
- Commitment
- Guarantee
- Pledge

Understanding your audience

Different people have different ways of thinking, of processing information. When giving a speech, be aware of your own way of processing information. Don't assume everyone thinks like you, or is persuaded by the same type of information. Make sure you offer other ways of approaching the subject matter, too. Here are some of the most common spectra –

Internal/external

- Some people are *internally* driven, they just know that what they think or feel to be right *is* right. Motivated by phrases such as: 'It's up to you.'
- *External* people want to know that other people also think it is right, they need external validation of their views. Motivated by phrases such as: 'You'll find your customers really appreciate this.'

Generalities/specifics

- *Generalities* – Some people prefer to see the big picture and are bored by detail. Motivated by: 'in general'; 'essentially.'
- *Specifics* – Specific people want detail – without them your speech will seem, to them, superficial and unconvincing. Motivated by: 'exactly'; 'Lets drill down to the detail on this.'

Proactive/reactive

- *Proactive* – Some people prefer to be proactive, they want to put their stamp on what's going on – to call the shots. Motivated by: 'Lets go for it.'
- *Reactive* – Reactive people prefer to react to the views of others. Motivated by: 'We need to look at this from every angle.'

Similarity/difference

- *Similarity* – These people don't like change, they usually like the familiar, they tend to blend in. Motivated by: 'The same, only better.'
- *Difference* – People who like difference want to mark themselves out from the crowd, they want new experiences. Motivated by: 'Unique'; 'Lets change the script.'

Options/procedures

- *Options* people feel confined by rigid rules, they want scope to express themselves, they see flexibility as a virtue. Motivated by: 'The possibilities are endless.'
- *Procedures* people feel safest when they know exactly where they are and what is expected of them. They think that options people are all over the place! Motivated by: 'First things first'; 'Lets go logically, step by step.'

Towards/away from

- *Towards people* are enthusiasts, if you want to persuade a towards person you will need to build their hopes and dreams. They tend to be optimists. Motivated by: 'We've got to think big.'
- *Away from people* – these people are distrustful of hope and dreams, they want reassurance that things won't go wrong, they want solutions to problems. Motivated by: 'We've got to be realistic about this.'

Different senses

Research suggests that we all have a dominant sense, and this is the sense on which we rely most to interpret the world.

For example, for some people their *sight* is the most important sense. They are very aware of their surroundings, the colour of a room, light and shade.

Those for whom *hearing* is the dominant sense will be very sensitive to sound (they are very aware of music playing in the background, of a radio that is not tuned in properly).

Other people are kinaesthetic, i.e. they like to touch and feel things – so the texture of cloth is important to them, they may be particularly sensitive to heat and cold.

As a presenter, you can use these senses to help people understand the message. If you express your message in language that appeals to the senses, it will be more easily absorbed.

For example:

- 'Can you see what I mean? I hope this is clear.'
- 'Can you hear what I am saying? Does it sound right to you?'
- 'Does this feel right to you? Can you pick up what I'm saying?'

Words that get through to visual people

- Light
- Bright
- Show
- See
- View

(e.g. 'Let's *show* them we mean business.')

Words that get through to aural people

- Attune
- Loud
- Hush
- Sound
- Listen

(e.g. 'We have got to get our message across *loud* and clear.')

Words that get through to kinaesthetic people

- Feel
- Touch
- Handle
- Soft
- Chaffing

(e.g. 'We must *pull* these people into the twenty-first century.')

9
Visual aids

- Props
- Overhead projector
- PowerPoint (using a data projector)
- Flip chart
- Other visual aids (display boards, albums, publicity material)

Props

'Real' props

Taking along an example of what you are talking about is a very good way of creating interest and aiding understanding. Props make the subject more real, they change the pace of the talk, they are memorable.

Police presenters almost always take handcuffs, body armour and extending truncheons with them. The speaker uses them to demonstrate aspects of police work, and the audience can pass them round, try them out. (Police speakers are often a 'prop' themselves – they tend to go in full uniform, even the plainclothes officers!)

When preparing your presentation, consider whether there is anything – a piece of equipment, an example of something your organisation makes, a typical example of an artefact from your field – that you could introduce to good effect.

Examples

Aleya was giving a talk about Sudanese refugees living in East London – she brought along some examples of Sudanese fabric, and some cooking utensils both to provide some visual references for the audience and also to explain the importance of familiar things for a community far from their country.

Jim was explaining to a tenants group about the gardening service's programme for cutting the grass and keeping weeds down. He took along the spraying equipment they would be using.

'Symbolic' props

Symbolic props, or 'metaphor' props, are objects that you invest with a meaning. For example, you could hold up a glass half filled with water and say, 'Is this half full, or half empty?'

Almost anything can be invested with meaning in this way. Look around any room and you will see lots of objects that can be used. A pair of glasses, a mirror, a sheet of paper, a pen, a piece of fruit, even a waste paper basket.

The aim is to get the object to convey your key message.

Example

Jenny worked on Best Value in her local authority. She was giving a presentation to staff about the enormous changes that Best Value meant for the way they worked. She took with her a waste paper basket. She put it in the middle of the stage, and started to tear up pieces of paper and throw them in the bin. 'We've got to tear up the rule book and start again,' she said, 'Best Value is going to change what we do, why we do it and how we do it.'

Dos and Don'ts when using props

Do:

- Commit yourself to using the prop with confidence and a bit of 'showmanship' and drama (if you don't have confidence in it, nor will your audience)
- Think about when is the best time to introduce the prop
- Usually keep the prop covered, or in a place where it will not be noticed until you need it
- Hold it up so the whole audience can see it
- Be very clear why you are using it, explain this to your audience

Don't:

- Choose something too obscure or, in the case of symbolic props, something whose meaning is too difficult to decipher
- Choose something too small, so that the people at the back can't see it

Overhead projector

An overhead projector is one of the most familiar visual aids used by presenters around the world. It is low tech and relatively easy to use. But before you decide to use it, think hard – do you really need it? Would it be better to give a presentation where *you* are the main visual aid?

Advantages

The OHP is suitable for:

- Formal and informal settings (including training)
- Small to medium sized audiences (from, say, 5–100)
- Use in most countries – you take your transparencies, they provide the OHP
- It gives flexibility – if you need to shorten or change the order of your presentation
- Not much can go wrong (but take an extra bulb)

Disadvantages

- The tall arm of the projector can block vision, especially in a small room
- It is overly formal for very small groups

Using an OHP

1. Get the right acetates

Make sure you buy the right type of acetate for your printer.

- Laser printers will need laser printer acetates

- Photocopying requires photocopy acetates (laser printer acetates are usually OK, but check the box)
- Ink jet printers need ink jet acetates
- If you are handwriting your acetates, get the ones that say they are for hand writing, and use dry marker pens

2. Design your acetates carefully

- Design and print them landscape, not portrait. Use PowerPoint to help you design clear, readable acetates
- Use large print – 48pt for headings, 28–36pt for the bullet points
- Use a maximum of five bullet points per slide. Each bullet point should be short and punchy – two to five words for each bullet point
- Colour can work well on acetates – use strong colours. However, visually impaired people may find them difficult to see, it is therefore good practice to use black only printing.
- Pictures – even photographs – can sometimes work well, but the quality of the original needs to be good, and photos will not work if projected very large
- Don't overuse clip art!
- Think about downloading appropriate/arresting images from the internet

3. Projecting the image

- OHPs can be projected onto a plain white wall or a screen. Make sure the OHP is correctly positioned (think about the positioning – if you have a screen, the image is sometimes more easily viewed if it is at an angle into the corner of a room)
- Make sure the image is in focus (before you begin your talk) by adjusting the lens, using the knob on the side of the tall arm. Check that it is visible from all angles
- Make sure you stand in a place where you are not blocking the screen

4. Keeping your transparencies/acetates in order

Make sure your transparencies are in the correct order and that you can easily move from one to the next (try numbering them with a small number in the corner).

5. The OHP stand

It is best to use a special OHP stand or trolley with a flap each side on which you can put your acetates/transparencies. You pick up the acetate, put it onto the projector, then when you have finished with it, move it to the other side.

6. Your relationship to the slides

Make sure you can read the slides as they lie on the projector glass (you should not be turning your back to the audience, reading from the screen).

7. Pointing

Point to bullet points using a pointer or your finger. Point onto the acetate on the OHP – don't point to the image on the screen.

8. Switching on and off

The OHP should only be on if you have an acetate on it (don't leave it on with no image showing).

Place your first slide onto the projector before you begin speaking and only switch it on when you get to the subject matter on that slide.

If the OHP is very noisy (some older ones have very noisy fans) you may wish to switch it off between slides. Otherwise it is probably best to keep it on most of the time (unless you digress, and what is on the screen is not helpful).

Make sure the acetate that is projected onto the screen has the appropriate headings/signposts for what you are talking about at the time (it is very confusing for the audience if you are talking about something completely different).

9. Speaking to OHP slides

Use your OHP slides as signposts – not as a script. You should not read them word for word (unless you suddenly go blank – when you can 'recap' by reading through the slide, this will give you time to get your brain back into gear).

10. The 'reveal' technique

Some presenters (particularly teachers) gradually reveal the bullet points on the acetate by covering parts with a piece of paper. This rarely looks professional – better to sort your material into two or three separate short slides.

11. Charts

- Graphics (pie charts, bar charts, pictorial displays) can be used effectively, but they must be simple – so the audience can get the point at a glance. It is pointless to put up a detailed bar chart containing lots of complex material
- You should fillet the original information to show overall trends (e.g. a bar chart on which you have monthly information will probably need to be cut down to quarterly information – showing just, say, January, April, July, and October)
- Use contrasting colours to show differences (e.g. a chart showing men's and women's use of cars – you could use, say, red for men and blue for women). Also, use a felt tip pen (suitable for the type of acetate you are using) to put a ring round key bits of information as you speak to them
- Remember the rules for type size still apply – nothing smaller than 28pt!
- Take time for the audience to take in a chart – they will need at least a minute. Talk them through it in some detail – don't just leave it up and talk around it

PowerPoint

Using PowerPoint on a data projector is increasingly seen as the more professional option for visual aids. It is very easy to use and a 'core' presentation can be updated for a specific audience in a matter of minutes.

But be careful of 'death by PowerPoint'. People often feel they must use PowerPoint to demonstrate they are 'professional' – rather than seeing it as just another visual aid, which is only worth using if it supports your presentation and adds something to it. Avoid overusing animated effects – stick to one type of animation and do not use the sound effects that go with the animation. Remember – less is more!

Advantages

A PowerPoint presentation is good for:

- Most sizes of groups, formal and informal
- Reproduction is usually very good quality, easily readable at the back of a large hall
- Graphics, charts etc. can be 'built up' as you talk your audience through them
- Video/sound can be incorporated
- If the venue has all the necessary equipment, you can travel light (with just a floppy disk or CD ROM). This is particularly useful when there are a number of presenters all using PowerPoint – make sure there is time between presentations to load the floppy (or transfer all floppies onto the hard disk before the presentations start)

Disadvantages

- It is now so common that all presentations tend to have the same look and feel
- It can look too flashy in a very small meeting
- If the venue is very low tech, they may not have the equipment you need – in which case you will need to take a computer and data projector with you

- You need to check that the venue is using the same generation software (or later) as you are using
- The equipment can go wrong (so take acetates as well!)

Using PowerPoint

Setting up the equipment

If you are expected to set up the data projector/computer yourself, get to the venue early enough to set everything up beforehand. If there is a technician liaise with him/her in advance of the meeting (e.g. do you need to take your own laptop? Are they using the same generation of PowerPoint as you?).

You can normally project onto either a screen or a blank white wall. Most data projectors can be projected in daylight but some have a much brighter lamp than others and the image will be often be easier to read if you dim the lights.

Decide where you are going to stand – don't block the screen. If you are going to be walking around, make sure you have an infrared mouse (for clicking to change slides).

PowerPoint automatically makes titles 44pt type and text 32pt type. You can change the size – but be careful, these type sizes have been chosen as the default because they are easy to read.

Formatting your slides

PowerPoint (and other presentation packages) have a number of pre-designed templates. Some of these are very flashy and over the top.

It is usually best to get your designers to design a template for everyone in your organisation to use – a template design that carries your brand image (logo, colours, typeface). If you cannot get a template designed in this way, use the custom design section of PowerPoint to design a simple slide template yourself.

People with visual impairments will find black writing on a white background easiest to read. Introduce colour in the logo, design lines etc.

Pictures

It is easy to import photographs, cartoons and other pictures into your slides. Be very sparing with clip art – it can look very tacky. You can import pictures from the internet – as long as it is just for a one-off, non commercial use, copyright should not be a problem (but if in doubt you should check it out with your lawyers).

If you are using graphics (charts, graphs etc.) give your audience enough time to take them in.

Don't forget your audience

Make sure you maintain good eye contact with your audience, and that the PowerPoint presentation is a support (not the main event) – you are still your own best visual aid.

Training notes

If you are using PowerPoint in a training setting, you may wish to print out your slides three or six to a page.

Flip Chart

A flip chart is essential for training, and is extremely useful for participative workshops (for logging the discussion). A flip chart can be used effectively in almost any small group.

Advantages

- It needs very little advance preparation
- It encourages participation by validating the audience's contributions in an interactive session
- A flip chart enables you to log the progress of a discussion, and to record that progress in a way that everyone can see and share

Disadvantages

- It is not usually suitable for meetings with a formal agenda

- Some presenters are not good spellers (especially onto a flip chart)

Using a flip chart

1. Setting up

Before the session starts check that you have:

- Enough clean paper on the flip chart
- Pens that work (in different colours) – make sure they are dark enough to be read (yellow/orange/light green can be very difficult to read). People with visual impairment may prefer black writing on white flipchart paper.
- Blu-Tack (for fixing flip chart paper to the wall, so that the group can see what has been written up); Post-it™ notes (for people to stick up on flip charts if you are using them in audience participation sessions)

Decide what the audience will see on the flip chart before the presentation starts – are you going to have a welcome message, a blank sheet, or some key words for your presentation?

Decide where to place the flip chart.

> Are you right or left handed? This will dictate whether you stand to the right or left of the flip chart (right handed people to the left, left handers to the right) – you need to be able to write without standing right in front of the flip chart. Reach across the chart to write. As far as possible, retain eye contact with the audience.

2. Don't hug the flip chart

Don't hold on to the edge of the flip chart while you are presenting.

3. Writing on the flip chart

Write legibly. Be as tidy as you can. Use large writing. Print, but don't use all capital letters – they take longer to write and they are more difficult to read.

Use bullet points (•).

Use squared paper if you can, it helps you write straighter!

Other visual aids

Illustrating with visual aids

If you are talking about a government report or want to remind people you have a leaflet – show an example to your audience. Hold it high – pause and look at it yourself, then explain what it is.

Touchy feely visual aids

It can reinforce your message if the audience *touch* as well as *see* your visual aid. For example, an album with pictures can be passed around instead of projecting images on the screen.

Display boards

Display boards can be placed in the room and, during your talk, you can wander over to refer to them – all the time holding your audience's attention. Or you can put the display boards on the stage to 'claim the territory' and help you take command of the space (again, refer to them during your presentation).

Post-it notes

You can sometimes get audience participation by giving out blank Post-it notes and asking people to write something on them. For example, you could throw out a question and get people to write their response on the Post-it. Then everyone gets up and sticks their notes onto one of a number of flip charts (grouping similar answers).

Index

Compiled by Sue Carlton

About the author

Tess Woodcraft is an experienced presenter who works with individuals and organisations in the UK and internationally, helping them communicate more effectively.

Tess draws on a wide range of experience. As CE of a national charity, she made presentations in all conceivable settings – from small meeting rooms, conferences and seminars, up to and including London's Trafalgar Square.

She has been a radio and TV presenter working for Channel 4 and BBC and, as Head of Communications for a London Borough wrote speeches for officers and members.

Tess currently works with the Centre for Strategy and Communication and is part of the Centre's talented team of media and communication specialists.